BELLWETHER MEDIA • MINNEAPOLIS, MN

Note to Librarians, Teachers, and Parents:

Blastoff! Readers are carefully developed by literacy experts and combine standards-based content with developmentally appropriate text.

Level 1 provides the most support through repetition of high-frequency words, light text, predictable sentence patterns, and strong visual support.

Level 2 offers early readers a bit more challenge through varied simple sentences, increased text load, and less repetition of high-frequency words.

Level 3 advances early-fluent readers toward fluency through increased text and concept load, less reliance on visuals, longer sentences, and more literary language.

Whichever book is right for your reader, Blastoff! Readers are the perfect books to build confidence and encourage a love of reading that will last a lifetime!

This edition first published in 2007 by Bellwether Media.

Library of Congress Cataloging-in-Publication Data
McClellan, Ray.
Concrete mixers / By Ray McClellan.
p. cm. – (Blastoff! readers) (Mighty machines)
Summary: "Simple text and supportive images introduce young readers to concrete mixers. Intended for students in kindergarten through third grade."
Includes bibliographical references and index.
ISBN-10: 1-60014-044-0 (hardcover : alk. paper)
ISBN-13: 978-1-60014-044-0 (hardcover : alk. paper)
1. Concrete mixers–Juvenile literature. I. Title. II. Series. III. Series: Mighty machines (Bellwether Media)

TA439.M225 2006
629.225–dc22 2006007212

Printed in the United States of America.

Table of Contents

A **concrete** mixer
is a big truck.
It carries and mixes
cement.

KIMBLE

A concrete mixer
has a **cab**.
A driver sits
in the cab.

cab
USDOT
NO RIDERS
299
299

A concrete mixer
has a **drum**.
The drum holds
the cement
and sand.

drum

The drum turns
and turns.
It mixes the
cement, sand,
and water
to make concrete.

MORAINE

The concrete flows down the **chute**.

chute

A worker
moves the chute
back and forth.

The concrete
mixer helps us
build houses.

MACK

Concrete mixers
help us make
tall buildings.

Can you tell what
a concrete mixer
helped build
in this picture?

Glossary

cab—a place for the driver to sit

cement—a type of glue; cement is mixed with sand and water to make concrete.

chute—the part of a concrete mixer that the concrete flows down

concrete—a hard and strong construction material

drum—a metal container on concrete mixers

To Learn More

AT THE LIBRARY

Eick, Jean. *Concrete Mixers.* Eden Prairie, Minn.: The Child's World, Inc., 1998.

Randolph, Joanne. *Concrete Mixers.* New York: Powerkids Press, 2002.

Williams, Linda D. *Concrete Mixers.* Mankato, Minn.: Capstone Press, 2004.

ON THE WEB

Learning more about mighty machines is as easy as 1, 2, 3.

1. Go to www.factsurfer.com
2. Enter "mighty machines" into search box.
3. Click the "Surf" button and you will see a list of related web sites.

With factsurfer.com, finding more information is just a click away.

Index

The photographs in this book are reproduced with the permission of: Mack Trucks, Inc., front cover, p. 17; R. I. Carr, Ph.D., P.E., p. 5; Jim Pruitt, p. 7; Terje Rakke/Getty Images, p. 9; McNeilus Companies, Inc., p. 11; Francois Etienne du Plessis, p. 13; Christina Richards, p. 15; Paul Cowan, p. 19; Michelle Pedone/ Getty Images, p. 21.